Alex Gildzen

OHIO TRIANGLE

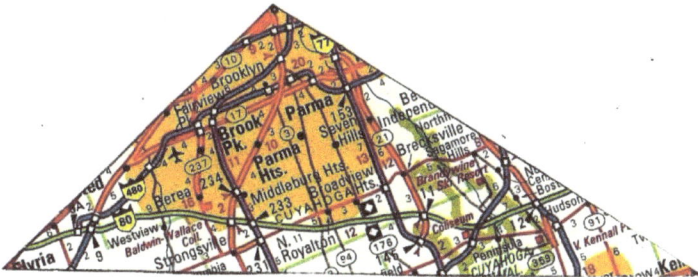

Ohio Triangle

Contents:

Published 25 April 2015
the author's 72nd birthday
as Crisis Chronicles #59
ISBN: 978-1-940996-19-6

Crisis Chronicles Press
3344 W. 105th Street #4
Cleveland, Ohio 44111 USA
crisischronicles.com
ccpress.blogspot.com
facebook.com/crisischroniclespress

Point A: Elyria

STRADDLING THIRD ST

in my imagination
I stand in the middle of the street
I point this way to the library
& that way to the Y

the roads I chose as a man
all startd here

the library was a stone mansion
with turret & balconies
& wraparound porch
I was as lost in its books
as in bodies
in locker room
across the street

a church bought the library
& knockd it down
(so much for churches)
years later the Y
was torn down too

but because I'm walking
in my imagination
both buildings stand proud

I point this way to my head
& that way to my heart

for the rest of my life
I'm in the middle of Third St

MORNING CANTATA

train whistling past General Industries
wakes me in my boyhood bedroom

Dad's snore is base line
clock's metronome numbers my pulse

cars drone down Broad St
while I await twack of Plain Dealer on porch

I flail under sheets
hearing a morning long ago:

Mom hiding Disney figurines
around living room

& later telling her little boy
they were left by the Easter bunny

musics past & present
crash in my ears

till tears blotch wrinkles
under my eyes

time to get up   gas griddle
for Dad to flip flapjacks

ELY PARK

from my bench
I see what I saw

Duke Ellington emerges
from hotel no longer there

Lila Lee walks by
history of film on her fragile shoulders

& right there by courthouse steps
I stand & wave back at JFK as he speeds toward Dallas

on this gray september morning
I look past sprays of water in central fountain

to town hall that's stood there since 1867
(Sherwood Anderson walkd past it on way to paint factory)

Thomasson's Potato Chip truck glides down Broad
past law offices that used to be the Rivoli

in other direction I see men in hardhats lay brick
for 6th floor of a justice center rising from rubble of the Y

I see young people at a picnic table
near Civil War monument & wonder

if in 40 years any of them will return to this park
& see me sitting here today

WINTER OF ONE HUNDRED INCHES OF SNOW

8 miles from Lake Erie
Elyria attracts snow
like cowpies flies

each morning
of this visit
back to Winckles St

I start day
wiggling into Dad's boots
pulling down woolen cap

it mite be fun
to make fresh tracks
on a trek to Cleveland St

instead I tend
to filial tasks
pushing a broom

till snow white
turns
pavement gray

I remember
a winter perhaps
a half century ago

when snow
seemd to reach
my waist

then magic
now burden
times change

this snow
feels heavier
each morning

sweeping it away
clears mind
cleans memory

I am the me
I was
& am

& now
snow
returns

FORD AT CASCADE PARK

Dad's old Chevy
wd slow   burp   stop
then the magic

that car wd seem
to float thru water
to other side

in my middle years
I'd cross the ford again
in my mind

boy's trip forward
becomes
man's journey back

just as the river
never stops
I'm always crossing

BLACK RIVER

never knew why
they calld it that

always seemd
brown to me

maybe when
Wyandot

campd
beside it

the river
was clean

a mirror
for the air

VIEW FROM THE PORCH

on the swing
Mother spots
chipmunk & squirrel
Betty next door
every car that turns
on to Winckles St

since all politics
is local
she's the mayor
of the block
& knows
her constituents
well

she tells
me stories
of each
who pass

then goes inside
to stir stew
she shares
with half
the neighbors

TOM MAHL REMINDS ME

squirrel tail on antenna
parallel with Winckles St
as Dad races
from Garford School
to home
Tom on one running board
me on the other
glee on our faces

MISS RADACHY

what luck
      led me
            at 11
                  to her class

she shot
      music
            into the air

opend
      our eyes
            to art

she never came to Winckles St
but in mud of memory
I see her boost me up that willow
to carve first lines in bark

LIVING WITH THE DEAD

Aunt Sophie's shortsnorter
bills from many countries
she taped together during the war

a favorite thing of mine
so I brought it to Eastern Heights
for "show & tell" in Miss Radachy's class

she signd a wrinkld lira
& on that same day
nearly 60 years ago

one of my classmates
wrote her name in green ink
beside the face of a small girl

"Susan Kirby"
writ boldly
with a flourish beneath

I remember dancing with her
just before we reachd our teens
& gossip between classes

at our junior high graduation dinner
she read the class will
which mentiond my writing

& then in our second month
of high school
Susan was dead

Asian flu   they sd
& we cried for her
& for ourselves

I walkd alone
to funeral home
& stood alone

beside her casket
she was the first my age
I'd seen dead

& for years I kept seeing her
eyes closed
on that pillow

with time dead Susan
meant more to me
than she had alive

I still dance with Susan
on my portal in the dark
& on Santa Monica pier

I twirl her around edges
of the medina in Tangier
& under a Barcelona moon

she whispers the class will
in my ear
allowing me to write

now so many friends dead
but
you always remember the first

GERMANS IN THE ATTIC

Dad's feet burn
it isn't neuropathy
but the thugs up there
aiming lasers at him

he hobbles
to utility room
raises his cane
& shouts
"stop it   godammit"
then goes out
to work
in his garden

WEARING MY HIGH SCHOOL VEST

what dust must rest
in ridges of that corduroy
& memories of more
than a half century

its green & brown lines
still form squares
while my lines
whir & jig

were I to know
when I wore it then
what I know now
how wd life change

cars still crash
loves dash & walls fall
but here I am
smiling in an old vest

THE CAMERA THAT LOOMS
OVER DOWNTOWN

for a half century
a shop
across from Ely Park
had a sign
with a giant camera

parents told their children
to be good
because that camera
recorded all they did

if only that were true
we'd have the real history
of the city
who met whom
in the park
& why

but shop closed
camera taken down
& all that history
it didn't record
slippd away

WAKING IN MY BOYHOOD HOME
FOR FIRST TIME
WITH NEITHER PARENT THERE

silence

EATING ELYRIA

back home in Santa Fe
I fix a salad
with produce
from garden
Sal plantd for Mom

tomatoes
green pepper
cucumber

each bite a memento mori
I chew the past
swallow tales told for decades

earth in which we grew
becomes dust with which we end

in front of Loomis Camera Shop

Point B: Cleveland

WAITING FOR WASCO

there's a Cleveland that only lives in memory
Santa Claus at Higbee's
tallest xmas tree in the world at Sterling Lindner's
Vera "the hat check chick" at a hotel that keeps changing its name
there's a Cleveland that only lives in memory
Bob Hope telling jokes at Cain Park
d.a. levy reading poems at Western Reserve
Judy Henske setting fire to a song at La Cave
there's a Cleveland that only lives in memory
Asphodel Bookshop is now a hotel room
Hippodrome Theater dead as Rock Hudson who I saw at a premiere there
China Lane mov'd down the street & into oblivion

but this morning I'm back in Cleveland
older than a ghost I walk down wet Euclid
from Playhouse Square to Tower City
in the bowels of Terminal Tower
I buy another book abt the Black Dahlia
watch water play in fountains
a man passes with bags of balloons
I consider seeing a movie
that spoofs those Rock & Doris pictures of my youth
I follow a handsome man to Caribou Coffee

I'm back in Cleveland
feeling as young as that school boy from Elyria getting off the train
details change as often as hemlines
but this city outlives torso killers & burning rivers
& I'm still here & still writing abt this city
& waiting to meet a new generation of Cleveland poets

ALL IN THE EYE

a friend in Brooklyn writes
he saw a movie
filmd in "ugly cleveland"

why shd that hurt?
I grew up an hour away
Cleveland wasn't home

maybe it's the boy in me
whose skin tingld
seeing Terminal Tower

once world's second tallest building
700 feet of beaux-art concrete & steel
casting a shadow on Lake Erie

that kind of hard-on you don't forget
so every time I visit Cleveland
I gaze up at it & tingle again

even here in the desert of my final years
when I go to bed the boy in me
turns to my nite table

to gaze up at
an antique souvenir
from beautiful Cleveland

a tiny Terminal Tower
casts its shadow
as I go to sleep

ALONE IN CLEVELAND

no Wasco so
dinner plans dumpd

I walk from hotel
to Greek Isles to find it
no longer there

on way back
I cut thru the Arcade
under its glass arch
time becomes a jumble

can it be 40 years
since I bought my first book
from Jim Lowell here?

I sit at end of stairs
around corner from that
other famous bookshop
the one Hart Crane hauntd

I look up at gilt balconies
& there he is

he's alone in Cleveland
I'm alone in Cleveland

I wink at him & he smiles
we meet at the Euclid entrance

"permit me to be
yr sailor for the nite"

he looks nervously both ways
then takes my hand
& kisses it

next morning
on way to airport
I glance at the spot
touchd by his lips

I see a word

now every nite I'm alone
I see that word
& the lips that left it
I see Hart Crane in the Arcade
smiling at me

& that word jumps
to paper
& I'm not alone
anymore

WEST SIDE MARKET

pierogies
Hungarian sausage
dark cherry strudel

sometimes
memory lives
on the tongue

TRACING THE PLACES OF D.A. LEVY

on the monitor
I see
Larry Smith's color pictures
of residences
from downstairs apartment
on Denison
next to the Kools sign
to box on Tuxedo
& brick building near West Side Market
to death site ruins

top floor
corner apartment
on Wymore
last place
to hold the breath
of a poet
building condemnd today
like levy's poems 40 years ago

but breath of lines
lingers in bare hallway
escapes into East Cleveland nite
opens gates
waits for new sun

a poet walkd here
tracing the places
clears ears
to hear
pries eyes
to see

DAY AFTER I LEARND DANIEL THOMPSON DIED
I saw a movie made in Cleveland

there was Michael Jeter (dead now too)
in front of a pierogie stand & Terminal Tower

there were Tremont streets Wasco walks
& a bus right out of my boyhood

& background music
by one of the men of Devo

the older I get the more this happens
this accumulation of layers

it can be spring in Santa Fe
white clematis blooming in my adobe courtyard

but my nose knows Ohio smells
lilac in Elyria   dandelion in Medina

& what I calld the sperm tree
on Kent's front campus

funny how I mark a decade in high desert
by writing poems abt another state

when I was a boy Dad wd drive over the ford
in Cascade Park to reach the bear den

those big brown animals wd piss
& yawn in their dark dank prison

bears haven't been there for years
but not long ago I crossd that ford again

splash of water on underbelly of car
how those bears wd paw their bars

all that Ohio is alive in me as dead men
remind me we are what we were

SHORT VINCENT

a street of 500 feet
its day was gone
before my nites

but on boyhood trips
I'd walk behind Hollenden
to that quick block
where notes of
Bobby Short at Kornman's
Dorothy Donegan at Theatrical Grill
hung in the air
where strippers
dancd for the mob
where Judy Garland
came for highballs & jazz

that was before
I ever heard Little Jimmy Scott
who must've felt like shit
walking past those marquees
on his way to the hotel
when he was a shipping clerk
instead of an angel

SERGEANT GILDZEN

sun's swallowd
by sharp edges
of Frank Gehry building
visible from Dad's window
at University Hospital

old soldier
strappd to bed
held captive
by Germans
but he outsmarts them
he will not swallow
he will not be taken
alive

DEAD POETS DAY

21 july 2010

1. d.a. levy

mountains
on his gravestone
instead of
Terminal Tower

2. Hart Crane

his statue
at Case Western Reserve
moved
behind library
but Hart
doesn't mind
he gazes
at Museum of Art
Gehry building
& that field
where anything
can happen at nite

3. Daniel Thompson

I walk from
Terminal Tower
down Daniel's Way
happy
that Cleveland
names its alleys
for poets

with Hart Crane statue on Dead Poets Day
[photo by John Burroughs]

Point C: Kent

STANDING ROCK

it's there in middle of the river
that place where Indians leapt

but I tend to think of things
which took its name

a press young poets of long ago
felt wd anoint them with fame

a cemetery where writer & porn star
share same green blanket

the more I think the more
of a muddle it becomes

the Haymaker buried in the cemetery
was subject of the poet of the press

that's how my life unfolds
rocks standing here turn up there

now that I'm old
it's tough to be surprisd

I expect letters from people
I knew decades ago

I wander cemeteries & find stones
of those whose voices I still hear

I suspect if I jumpd onto Standing Rock
I'd discover my blood staining it

what happens in poems
either already happened or will

the more I live the more
of a muddle it becomes

so I need the poem
to make sense of it all

BLIND OWL
(1964-65)

Biff & Buzz & Buffy
singing
at "the sanctuary
of living
folk music"

in alley
across from
Commercial Press

we wore
all black then
& drank
hot cider
with cinnamon sticks

we were
cool
& laughd at
frat boys
in their
skinny ties

OFF CAMPUS

1.

        Garret
        334 South Willow
        (june 1964 - dec 1965)

across former attic
Jim Hailey's room

once he came over
wearing only a towel
he sat & let
it slip open

I didn't know
what to do
so kept on talking

2.

        Lot 93
        State Trailer Park
        (jan – mar 1966)

short time
renting Smullen's trailer

it became
grad student hub
Bob & Betty & George & I
drilling the canon

& once
after everyone left
a pounding on my door
but

I wasn't ready
to open it

3.

       Apt 310
       548 East Summit
       (apr – sept 1966)

one nite
Pakistani roommate
walkd in
on friend
& me
pants down
on living-
room rug

weeks later
he skippd
out in
the nite
with a
classmate's wife

CALDO VERDE SOUP

potato
cabbage
spinach
pepperoni

made by Eddie
servd by Bert
at Stag Bar

winters I walkd
there for that

spoon to bowl
bridge back

FRIDAY NITE AT THE BARS

at Walter's the rum
in my rum & coke
was so cheap
it tastd medicinal

not like Bacardi's
liquid sugar
servd at Friar Tuck

but Walter's was where
painters & poets hung
we'd get half tankd
before drifting next door
to the cave calld The Kove
to hear Numbers Band
then back to Walter's
to finish the job

if I cd still stand
& felt like boys
I'd stumble to Ray's
to talk to strangers

once at a big place
with many names
I got into a fight
leaving part of a tooth
on the pavement

those lost nites
are a silent movie
playd at wrong speed
the me I see
had hair & gall
balls enough
to joke with jocks

but most nites
I was alone
at last call

STOPHER HALL

when I saw
my dorm fallen
I wantd to search
the rubble
for a linoleum square
from the floor
of room 321
or a manila block
from the showers
I wantd to hold
my memories
but I walkd on

ART & POLITICS

no one heard
Smithson's beam break

but rifles of may
remain in our ears

HOLLYWOOD COMES
TO KENT

Paul Newman
ate at Jerry's Diner

Sylvia Sidney
checkd out
of Kent Motor Inn

Sam Fuller
checkd in
same room

May Allison
came to remember
silence with
Lois Wilson
in town
to do a play

Lily Tomlin
did somersaults
at a press conference

but the story
most remember best
is young
W. C. Fields
stuck in town
when his troupe
went broke
& he left his trunk
in exchange
for a train ticket

SOMEWHERE IN MY HEAD
it's always Halloween in Kent

Craig sits on my lap
making up my face

Henry   no matter his costume
has a glass in hand

Donna laughs madly
while David hugs everyone

now when that day comes
I no longer dress up

I have pictures in albums
& a charcoal eye pencil in a drawer

THIS THEN IS THE WHEEL

1968

at Stag Bar
d.a. levy plays
with his rigatoni

he gives his meatball
to Mary Leed

poetry isn't art
he tells us
it's communication

1971

on the Commons
Allen Ginsberg squeezes
harmonium
while singing Blake

thru crowd
of seatd students
comes Gary Snyder
to surprise
his old friend

performance
stops
for joyful embrace

1976

in Twin Lakes
Thomas Meyer dives

into pool

our bare bodies
touch under water

Jonathan Williams reaches
for his Rollei

1981

on Morris Rd
James Broughton works
on a poem
while
Joel Singer
dices avocado
for our cheese omelet

we laugh
during dinner

then they go
hand in hand
to bed

ALGESA'S TABLE

painter & critic
poet & prince
she & Joe
assemble
the cast

hors d'oeuvres
among books
in livingroom

a carnival of ideas
moves to table
for feast

delirium
of gustation
that feeds
mind & body

her greatest work of art

GUEST OF HONOR

in a kilt
he walkd
from special Jack the Ripper edition
of *The Globe*
to a copy of
The Great Harry Thaw Case
& the final piece
in the exhibition
his *Black Dahlia*

he charmd fans
thru dinner
then gave a speech

but when
all guests were gone
James Ellroy
left the library
liftd his head
& howld
like a dog

THOSE WHO CAME TO MY DOOR

they won't be
in the biography
no one will write

but their kisses
light my path
to the end

I dare not name them
for fear of
leaving one out

each found a way
to Morris Rd
& my bed

each left
with a poem
written in sweat

THRU GLASS BLOCKS IN VENICE CAFÉ
I see a city that was

Kent is still there
Dean Keller still prints broadsides
on the Chandler & Price in his basement
my old letters remain in boxes
at top of the library
but 2 decades separate me
from the city in which I lived
for almost 33 years

so thru those glass blocks
what I see is no longer clear
images real but with soft edges

there I am reading my poems
in the train station
before it became a restaurant
& there's Julia Waida smiling
as she brings out her kettle cake
& Howard Vincent in Harpoon Hall
trading quips with Robert Duncan
& Devo playing at a friend's party

thru those glass blocks
Kent is what was

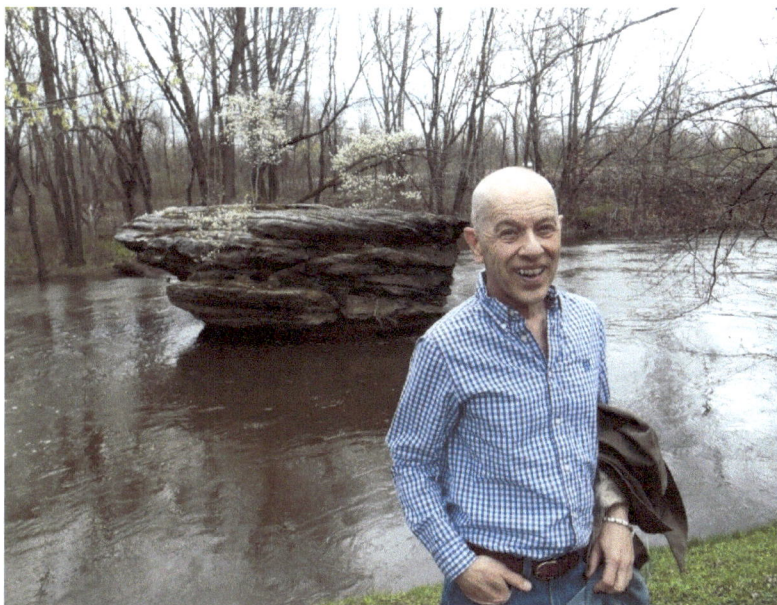

at Standing Rock
[photo by Lainard Bush]

Epilog

POINTS ON A MAP

in the movie of my life
I am the star
legendary ladies of the screen
make cameos

Lila Lee
after dinner
with my parents
on Winckles St
asks if I can put
some whisky
in her coffee

Lana Turner
at a premiere
in Cleveland
floats
on white ostrich feathers

Sylvia Sidney
at Stag Bar
in Kent
remembers
her first film

points on a map
locate
people in a life

my Ohio triangle
points me
to streets & alleys
bars & beds

full of faces

places collide
where I am now
is where I have been
I keep saying it
as final reel
nears

Some of these poems have appeared in *Arroyo Chamisa*, *Big Bridge*, *Street Value*, *Deep Cleveland Junkmail Oracle*, *Thee Flat Bike*, *RFD*, *Saturday's Poem* as well as in the anthology *Drivvin* (Green Panda Press, 2011).

An early version of the Elyria section was published as a chapbook by Crisis Chronicles Press in 2009. We also released a revised illustrated edition via Kindle in 2013. The Cleveland section was published as a chapbook by Crisis Chronicles Press in 2013.

"Dead Poets Day" was published as a broadside by NightBallet Press in 2011.

"Those Who Came to My Door" and "Thru Glass Blocks in a Venice Café" were published as broadsides by 48th Street Press in 2014.

He was born in California, first walked in Texas and now lives in New Mexico but Alex Gildzen spent the majority of his life as a resident of Ohio. He was two weeks old when he arrived in Lorain. When his father returned from the war in Europe the family moved to Elyria. He began visiting Cleveland as a child. Following graduation from Elyria High School he went to Kent State University where he was student, teacher and librarian. In 1993 Kent presented him with the President's Medal for "extraordinary and unique service" to the university. The same year the Ohio Arts Council honored him with the Ohioana Citation in the field of humanities and education.

So far from Crisis Chronicles Press

CC#67 — *Bookmobile: From the Library of Jesus Crisis* by David S. Pointer

CC#66 — *Thunderclap Amen* by Dianne Borsenik

CC#65 — *Cutting the Möbius* by Jonathan Thorn

CC#64 — *Be Closer for My Burn* by Robin Wyatt Dunn

CC#63 — *#ThisIsCLE: An Anthology of the 2014 Best Cleveland Poem Competition* by various authors

CC#62 — *I Don't* by Bree

CC#61 — *HOLDING STORIES in YOUR HANDS: Narrative Poems and Poetic Narratives* by Elise Geither

CC#60 — *The Night Market* by D.R. Wagner

CC#59 — *Ohio Triangle* by Alex Gildzen

CC#58 — *Poems for Explosion* by John G. Hall

CC#57 — *City of Tents: Poems About the Occupy Movement and Other Items Taken From the News* by Martin Willitts, Jr.

CC#56 — *Irises Made of Moth Wings* by Christian O'Keeffe

CC#55 — *Oct Tongue -1* by Mary Weems, John Swain, Steven Smith, Lady [Kathy Smith], Shelley Chernin, John Burroughs and Steve Brightman

CC#54 — *Songs in the Key of Cleveland: An Anthology of the 2013 Best Cleveland Poem Competition* by various authors

CC#53 — *Cut Me Free* by Ben Heins

CC#52 — *In Bold Blackness: Selections* by Jami Tillis

CC#51 — *Sunshine Liar* by Ryan Swofford

CC#50 — *YES, but....* by Martin Burke

CC#49 — *Every Bird, To You* by Sarah Marcus

CC#48 — *13 Ways Of Looking At Lou Reed* by Steve Brightman

CC#47 — *secret letters* by j/j hastain

CC#46 — *Cleveland: Point B in Ohio Triangle* by Alex Gildzen

CC#45 — *Rain and Gravestones* by John Swain

CC#44 — *Cheap and Easy Magazine, volume 1* by 36 contributors

CC#43 — *Bus Riders in the Storm* by Cee Williams

CC#42 — *My America* by Cee Williams

CC#41 — *The Everyday Parade / Alone With Turntable, Old Records* by Justin Hamm

CC#40 — *Howl for My Family in April* by Mary C. O'Malley

CC#39 — *Body Voices* by Kevin Reid

CC#38 — *the melody, I swear, its just around that way: volume 2* by Bree

CC#37 — *Grand Slam* by Alan S. Kleiman
CC#36 — *Red Hibiscus* by Heather Ann Schmidt
CC#35 — *Photograph* by Jackie Koch
CC#34 — *Queen of Dorksville* by Leah Mueller
CC#33 — *Angel* by Sandy Sue Benitez
CC#32 — *In Circles* by Ryn Cricket
CC#31 — *The Other Guy* by John Thomas Allen
CC#30 — *as she unbends* by Jolynne Hudnell
CC#29 — *Street maps for lost souls* by John Dorsey
CC#28 — *I Can Live with Death* by David B. McCoy
CC#27 — *The Wandering White* [broadside] by d.a. levy
CC#26 — *White Vases* by John Swain
CC#25 — *The Anarchist's Blac Book of Poetry* by Frankie Metro
CC#24 — *The Vigil* by Shelley Chernin
CC#23 — *This Is How She Fails* by Lisa J. Cihlar
CC#22 — *desire lines* by Chansonette Buck
CC#21 — *12 Poems* by Cee Williams
CC#20 — *Lens* by John Burroughs, a.k.a. Jesus Crisis [out of print]
CC#19 — *Primer for the Vanguard Youth* by RA Washington
CC#18 — *Only Human by Definition* by Jay Passer
CC#17 — *Rapid Eye Movement* by J.E. Stanley
CC#16 — *Grace, You Let the Screen Door Slam* by William
          Merricle
CC#15 — *the melody, I swear, its just around that way* by Bree
CC#14 — *Burnin' Shadows* by Kevin Eberhardt
CC#13 — *Fracture Mechanics/TRAP DOORS* by Michael Bernstein
CC#12 — *Unruly* by Steven B. Smith
CC#11 — *Blue Graffiti* by Dianne Borsenik
CC#10 — *Fever Dreams* by Yahia Lababidi
CC#9 — *Transient Angels* by Heather Ann Schmidt
CC#8 — *Identity Crisis* by Jesus Crisis
CC#7 — *Fuck Poetry* anthology by 40 authors [out of print]
CC#6 — *The Bat's Love Song: American Haiku* by Heather Ann
         Schmidt
CC#5 — *Suburban Monastery Death Poem* by d.a. levy
CC#4 — *Elyria: Point A in Ohio Triangle* by Alex Gildzen
CC#3 — *6/9 Improvisations in Dependence* by Jesus Crisis

CC#2 — *HardDrive/SoftWear* by Dianne Borsenik
CC#1 — *Bloggerel* by Jesus Crisis

And more titles coming soon by Susan A. Sheppard, Juliet Cook, Lyn Lifshin, George Wallace, Mark Sebastian Jordan, Eric Anderson, Margaret Bashaar, Kathleen Cerveny, Heather Ann Schmidt, Alinda Wasner, Kevin Ridgeway, Austen Roye, Richard M. O'Donnell, William Merricle, Catherine Criswell, Carolyn Srygley-Moore, Tracie Morell, Meg Harris, Steven Smith, Christopher Franke, Helen Shepard, Azriel Johnson, John Greiner, Esteban Colon, John Dorsey and Lisa Cihlar.

To get any Crisis Chronicles title, send ten US dollars to John Burroughs, 3344 W. 105th Street #4, Cleveland, Ohio 44111. Or purchase via PayPal to jc@crisischronicles.com. Please add a few dollars for international orders.

www.ingramcontent.com/pod-product-compliance
Lightning Source LLC
Chambersburg PA
CBHW051235090426
42740CB00001B/32